Birds of Canada

Einstein Sisters

KidsWorld

Common Loon

The common loon dives underwater to catch fish. It usually swallows the fish underwater.

Loons must **run across** the **water** before they can take off. They have to live on **big lakes** so they have **room to run.**

A loon's **legs** are far back on its **body**. That means it can't walk **very well.**

A **loon chick** can **swim** soon after it **hatches**. Sometimes chicks ride on their **mother's back.**

The ruby-throated hummingbird **beats its wings 55 to 75 times per second.** Its **tiny heart** beats up to **1200 times** per minute.

Only the male has a ruby red throat. The female's throat is white with some dark streaks.

Hummingbirds are **one of the only birds** that can fly **backwards**. They can also **hover**.

Hummingbirds **drink nectar** from flowers and **sugar water** from special **feeders**. They prefer **red or orange flowers**.

Bald Eagle

A pair of eagles builds a huge nest of sticks. They add to it every year. They make the largest nest of any Canadian bird.

A bald eagle isn't really bald. It gets its name from the white feathers on its head.

Bald eagles fly up to 3000 metres in the air. They can soar for hours using warm air currents.

Bald eagles
always live near water.
They eat mostly
fish.

Ruffed Grouse

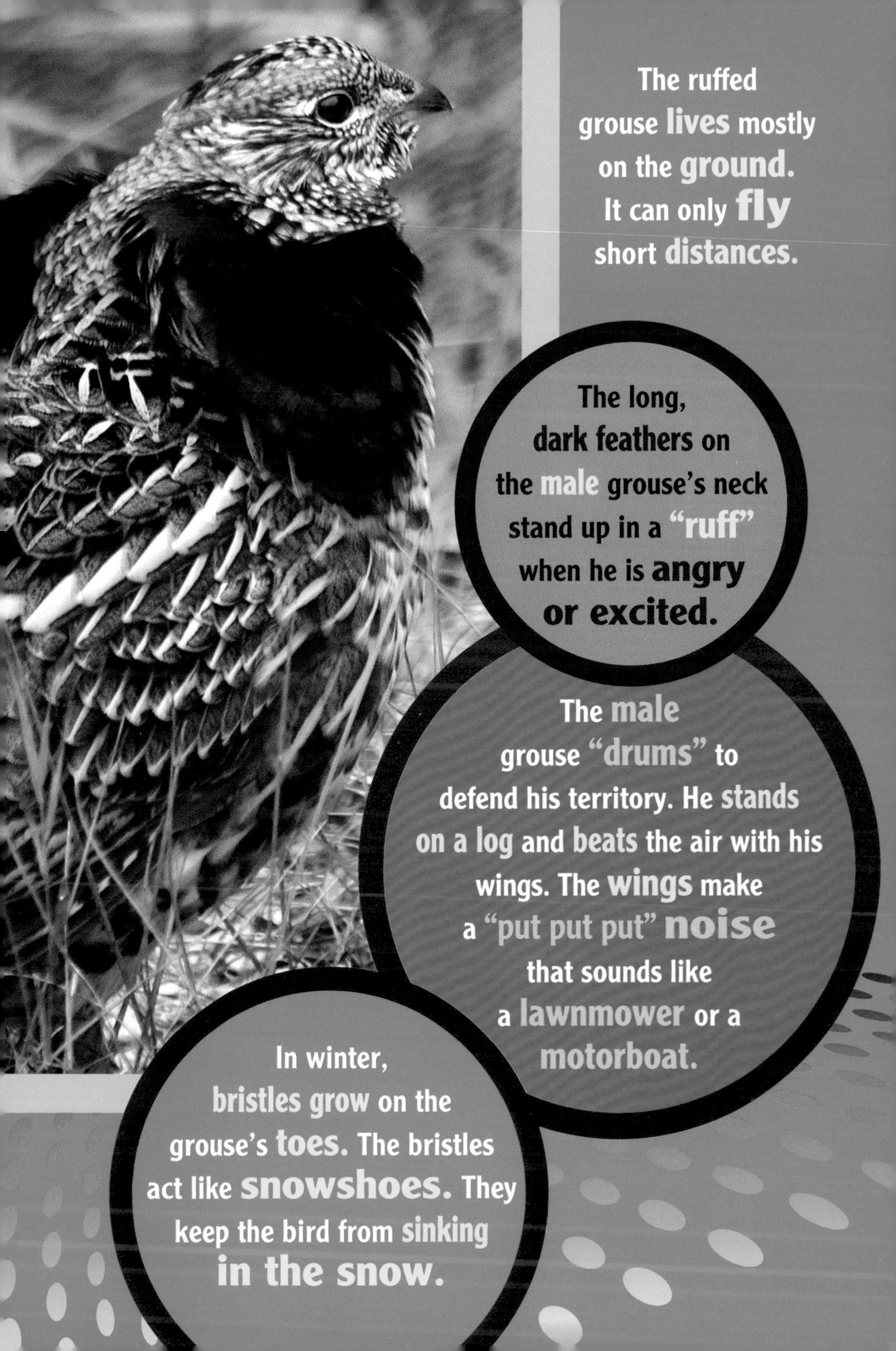

The ruffed grouse lives mostly on the ground. It can only fly short distances.

The long, dark feathers on the male grouse's neck stand up in a "ruff" when he is angry or excited.

The male grouse "drums" to defend his territory. He stands on a log and beats the air with his wings. The wings make a "put put put" noise that sounds like a lawnmower or a motorboat.

In winter, bristles grow on the grouse's toes. The bristles act like snowshoes. They keep the bird from sinking in the snow.

Belted
Kingfisher

The female kingfisher has a rusty brown "belt" across her chest.

Belted kingfishers always live near water. They eat mostly fish, crayfish and frogs.

Kingfishers don't make nests. They dig a burrow into an earthen bank.

The kingfisher's eyes are protected by a third eyelid. The eyelid closes when the bird dives into the water to catch a fish.

Red-winged Blackbird

The red-winged blackbird is one of the most common birds in Canada. You often see them sitting on top of cattails in marshes.

The male defends his territory from other blackbirds by **singing.** His song isn't very musical. It sounds like a **loud, raspy** "konk-a-ree."

The female blackbird is **streaky brown.** When she sits **on her nest,** she is camouflaged among the **cattails.**

The male's **bright red** shoulder patches are called "**epaulettes.**"

Black-capped Chickadee

You often see black-capped chickadees at backyard feeders. They are curious and friendly. A chickadee might even take seeds from your hand.

When it is cold, the chickadee fluffs out its feathers to trap warm air close to its body. At night, it lowers its body temperature to save energy.
Chickadees hide seeds to eat later. They can remember hundreds of hiding spots.
Chickadees are named for their "chick-a-dee-dee-dee" call.

Red-tailed Hawk

The red-tailed hawk is named for its brick red tail.

This hawk eats mostly mice, rabbits and ground squirrels. It can spot prey from hundreds of metres in the air.

Red-tailed hawks live in fields and grasslands. They like to perch on lone trees, utility poles and cliffs.

These **hawks** make a **screaming call** that sounds like **"keee-arrr."**

Male and female mallards look different. The male mallard has a shiny, green head. The female is brown.

A mallard is a kind of duck. A baby mallard is called a duckling.

Mallard

A duck's feet can't feel cold. It is comfortable walking on ice and swimming in cold water.

Mallards and other ducks swim well because of their **webbed feet.**

A blue jay's feathers aren't really blue. The feathers **reflect light**, making the bird look **blue.**

Blue Jay

Blue jays protect their nests by **dive-bombing intruders.**

The blue jay's **crest** usually lies flat against **its head.** The crest **stands up** when the bird is **excited** or **angry.**

Blue jays eat mostly acorns, nuts and seeds. They often carry food away and hide it so they can eat it **later.**

American Robin
The male robin has a bright red chest, but the female is more brownish.

Robins are one of the **earliest birds** to arrive in spring. Their **happy, musical song** sounds like "**cheerily cheer-up cheerio.**"

A robin often **stands still** and **turns its head** as if it is **listening.** It is really looking for **earthworms** moving **under the grass.** It tilts its head so it can see better.

Robins **eat worms** and **insects** in summer. In winter, they **fly south** to warmer places where they eat **mostly berries.**

The great blue heron is a wading bird. It stands in the water and waits for a fish to swim by, then it quickly grabs the fish and eats it.

Great Blue Heron

When a great blue heron flies, it holds its neck in an "S" shape.

The great blue heron is the **largest heron in Canada.** It stands about a metre high. That is as **tall as a child.**

Sometimes herons hunt in fields. There they catch mice and gophers to eat.

Tundra Swan

Tundra swans spend summers in the Arctic. In winter, they live on coastlines and lakes farther south.

Some people call this bird "whistling swan" because of the sound its wings make when it is flying.

Tundra swans sleep on water or ice in winter. To stay warm, they tuck their heads under their wings.
A tundra swan has a yellow patch in front of each eye.

Great Horned Owl

An owl can't move its eyes, so it has to turn its head. An owl can turn its head almost all the way around to the back.

Owls fly **very quietly** and swoop down on their **prey**. They eat **bugs, mice, snakes** and small **birds.**

Great horned owls **eat their prey whole.** Then they **throw up** pellets made of **bones and fur.**

This **owl** doesn't really have horns.
It has long feathers called "plumicorns"
that look like **horns**
or **ears.**

Common Tern

Common terns that live near the ocean drink salt water. They have special glands that remove the salt from the water.

In winter, the common tern has black legs, a black bill and a white forehead.

To catch fish, this tern flies high in the air. Then it dives into the water.

Terns always
live near water.
You can find them near
lakes, rivers, oceans
and marshes.

Red crossbills make a loud "jip-jip" call when they fly or perch.

Red Crossbill

The red crossbill uses its unusual beak to pry open spruce and pine cones so it can eat the seeds inside.

The male crossbill is orangey red. The female is greenish yellow.

The beaks of crossbills can be crossed in either direction.

Canada Goose

A **pair** of geese stays together all their lives. When the female goose is sitting on the **nest**, the male goose **stands guard**.

Flocks of Canada geese fly in a "V" shape. The geese **take turns** flying at the **front**.

The Canada goose makes a **honking sound.**

Even though they are **water birds**, **Canada geese** spend a lot of time **on land**. You can often see them on **lawns**, in **parks** and on **golf courses.**

American goldfinches are strict vegetarians. They eat mostly **thistle** and **dandelion seeds.**

American Goldfinch

Only the male goldfinch has a black cap, and he only has it in summer. The female's colours are duller.

Goldfinches weave their nests so tightly that they can hold water.

Flocks of goldfinches often sing together. Males even sing while flying.

Yellow Warbler

Some people call these brightly coloured birds "wild canaries." Only the male has reddish brown streaks on his breast.

Yellow warblers eat mostly insects and caterpillars, so you probably won't see them at your backyard feeder.

The male's musical song sounds like "sweet sweet sweet summer sweet."
Most songbirds, including yellow warblers, migrate at night.

Peregrine Falcon

The peregrine falcon is one of the **world's fastest birds.** When it **dives** to catch prey, it can reach 320 kilometres per hour. It mostly **eats birds** such as **ducks** and **pigeons.**

Peregrines usually nest on cliffs. In cities, they make nests on the **tops of tall buildings.**

The peregrine falcon is found on every continent except Antarctica.

The name peregrine means "wanderer." The peregrine falcon makes one of the longest migrations of any Canadian bird. Every winter, it flies to Mexico or South America.

Ring-billed Gull

The ring-billed gull is one of the most common gulls in Canada. You can see flocks of them on beaches and in fields. You can also find them in parking lots and landfills.

This gull isn't really a "sea gull." It is seen inland more often than other kinds of gulls.

Ring-billed gulls eat almost anything. They prefer fish, mice and insects, but they also eat garbage and french fries.

Gulls nest in large groups called "colonies." The largest colony is in the United States on Lake Ontario. It has about 160,000 birds.

Purple Finch

The purple finch is often described as "a sparrow dipped in raspberry juice."

Only the male finch is red. The female is greyish brown with white streaks.

Purple finches eat mostly seeds, buds and berries.

The purple finch crushes seeds with its thick bill. It uses its tongue to take out the kernels inside the seeds.

Spotted sandpipers always **live near water.** You can see them along streams and rivers, and also by **ponds, lakes** and **marshes.**

Spotted Sandpiper

The female lays the eggs, but the male takes care of them. He also takes care of the chicks when they hatch.

Spotted sandpipers teeter when they walk. They constantly bob their tails up and down.

In winter, the spotted sandpiper's breast is plain white.

Song Sparrow

Male song sparrows sing to **defend their territory** and to **attract females.** A young sparrow learns to sing by **listening** to his **father** or to **other males.**

The **streaks** on a song sparrow's **chest** often meet to **form** a **dark spot.**

When the **weather is cold,** song sparrows have to eat up to **4000 seeds an hour** to keep up their energy levels.

Song sparrows in **different parts** of Canada **sing different songs.** The **song sparrows** in each **region** have their own **"language."**

Downy Woodpecker

The downy woodpecker is the smallest woodpecker in **Canada.** You can see it at **backyard feeders,** in **parks** and in **forests.**

The **male** has a small, red **patch** on the **back of his head.**

A woodpecker uses its **long tongue** to get **insects** and **grubs** out of the **holes that it drills.** The tongue is covered with **sticky, glue-like saliva.**

Special feathers around the woodpecker's nostrils keep it from breathing in sawdust.

Common Raven

Some scientists think that ravens are as smart as chimpanzees and dolphins.
The common raven is an acrobatic flier. It can do rolls and somersaults in the air. It can even fly upside down.
Ravens mate for life. They can live as long as 50 years.
Ravens are about twice as big as crows. Ravens also have shaggy throat feathers.

Red-breasted nuthatches often move **headfirst down tree trunks.** They are looking for **bugs** in nooks and crannies in the bark.

Red-breasted Nuthatch

The red-breasted nuthatch nests in a hole in a tree trunk. It smears tree sap around the entrance to its nest to keep out ants and other intruders.

Nuthatches like bird feeders that have suet or peanut butter.

To open a hard-shelled nut, the nuthatch jams it into a crack in the bark of a tree. Then it hammers the nut with its beak to break it open.

Winter Wren

The little winter wren is the **loudest bird** for its size. Its song can be more than **10 seconds long.**

The male wren defends his territory by singing. His song tells other birds to stay away.

A winter wren often holds its short tail upright.

Winter wrens hide among thick underbrush in forests. They are difficult to see but easy to hear.

When waxwings eat berries, one bird will pluck a berry and pass it to another bird in the group.

Cedar waxwings like to live and eat together in large flocks. They often gather in trees with berries, especially mountain-ashes.

Cedar Waxwing
The name "waxwing" refers to the waxy red "drops" on the wings. These red spots get their colour from the berries that the birds eat.
Waxwings nest later than other songbirds so that berries will be ripe when the young birds hatch.

Killdeer

Killdeers are **shorebirds**. You often see them on **beaches** and lakeshores. They also live on lawns, **golf courses** and **sports fields**.

Killdeer **chicks** hatch with their eyes open. As soon as their downy **feathers are dry**, they run around looking for something **to eat.**

The killdeer is named for its call. It makes a loud "kill-dee" or "dee-dee-dee" sound.

When a person or animal comes too close to the killdeer's nest, the bird pretends to have a broken wing. It drags its wing on the ground and leads the predator away from the nest. Then the killdeer gives a loud call and flies away.

Barn Swallow

Barn swallows build their nests under bridges and house eaves. They also live in barns and abandoned buildings.

Barn swallows spend most of their time flying. They catch insects while in flight. They will even dip down to a lake to sip a mouthful of water while on the wing.

You can recognize a barn swallow by its forked tail.

To **make a nest,** barn swallows collect small balls of mud in their beaks. They **mix the mud with grass** and stick the balls **together.**

Printed in China

The Publisher: KidsWorld Books

Library and Archives Canada Cataloguing in Publication

Birds of Canada / Einstein Sisters.

ISBN 978-0-9940069-2-9 (pbk.)

1. Birds—Canada—Juvenile literature. I. Einstein Sisters, author

QL685.B5813 2015 j598.0971 C2015-901208-2

Cover Images: Front cover: American goldfinch, nigel/Flickr. *Back cover:* bald eagle, Comstock/Thinkstock; ruby-throated hummingbird, SteveByland/Thinkstock; blue jay, impr2003TS/Thinkstock.

Background Graphics: abstract background, Maryna Borysevych/Thinkstock, 9, 21, 33, 45, 55; abstract swirl, hakkiarslan/Thinkstock, 3, 19, 31, 43, 53; pixels, Misko Kordic/Thinkstock, 4, 6, 13, 14, 16, 25, 26, 27, 28, 35, 37, 38, 40, 46, 48, 49, 50, 59, 60, 62.

Illustration Credits: Gary Ross, 6, 8, 10, 13, 14, 17, 18, 20, 24, 26, 28, 31, 35, 39, 40, 42, 47, 48, 50, 52, 57, 62; Ted Nordhagen, 3, 4, 23, 33, 36, 45, 54, 59, 60.

Photo Credits: From Flickr: aecole2010, 38; Anthony Sokolik, 34–35; David Mitchell, 51a; fishhawk, 59; Jim the Photographer, 63; Kelly Colgan Azar, 58; Kevin Cole, 11; nigel, 37; Oregon Department of Fish and Wildlife, 16; Robert Engberg, 20–21; Rodney Campbell, 38–39; Ron Mead, 52–53; U.S. Fish and Wildlife Service, 51b. *From Thinkstock:* ca2hill, 41; CarolinaBirdman, 25; Cheryl Davis, 22–23; Comstock, 7; creighton359, 8–9; csterken, 29; erniedecker, 36; impr2003, 14–15; Juha Remes, 18–19; Michael Fitzsimmons, 19; Michael Vodiansky, 13; Ornitolog82, 56–57; PaulReevesPhotography, 12, 30–31, 48–49, 60–61; Purestock, 26–27; RyanVincePhotography, 41; SteveByland, 4–5, 21, 24, 54–55. *From Wikipedia:* Cephas, 44–45; Elaine R. Wilson, 32–33; Greg Hume, 17; John Picken, 2–3; Mdf, 42–43, 46; Mike Michael L. Baird, 10–11.

We acknowledge the financial support of the Government of Canada.
Nous reconnaissons l'appui financier du gouvernement du Canada.

Funded by the Government of Canada
Financé par le gouvernement du Canada | Canadä

PC: 38-3